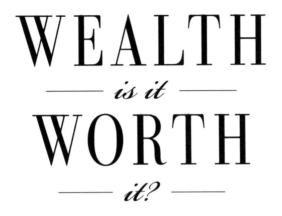

WEALTH
— is it —
WORTH
— it? —

WEALTH
— *is it* —
WORTH
— *it?* —

S. TRUETT CATHY

Founder of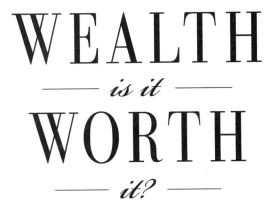

Contents

$\mathcal{F}$oreword

Ken Blanchard
Coauthor of *The One Minute Manager*® and *Leading at a Higher Level*

In the late 1990s I was trying to find a role model for a book I was writing about generosity. Norman Vincent Peale, the author of *The Power of Positive Thinking*, introduced me to Truett Cathy, the founder of Chick-fil-A, then a billion-dollar company that currently operates more than fifteen hundred restaurants in thirty-nine states and Washington, D.C. "He's one of the most generous people I know," Norman said.

As I got to know Truett, I saw what Norman meant. Here was a man who had solid values, a deep concern for others, and a passion for sharing not only his wealth, but also his time, talent, and touch. Truett operates twelve foster homes where hundreds of foster grandchildren have lived over the years. He started a summer camp for children and has handed out more than $26 million in scholarships to team members working in Chick-fil-A restaurants. He taught Sunday school to boys for more than sixty years, and he has created a foundation that will continue to touch young lives well into the future.

Truett allowed me to base the main character in our book *The Generosity Factor* on his life if, and only if, I changed the setting and situations so that people wouldn't think it was about him. He wasn't looking for recognition; he simply wanted to share what he'd learned with others.

Luckily for readers, Truett has now written a book that tells his real-life stories, revealing the ups and downs of building his company and sharing the wisdom he's gleaned along the way. The book asks an important question: Is money worth the trouble it takes to attain it? Is it worth the trouble it can bring if you happen upon it through good fortune? His answer is profound and just what you'd expect from a man famous for his generosity:

Wealth is worth it only if you give it away.

Thanks, Truett, for sharing your stories and insights and most of all, for being a role model for the rest of us.

Ken

Introduction

Dave Ramsey

Host of *The Dave Ramsey Show* and best-selling author
of *The Total Money Makeover*

I've had the blessing—and the challenge—of talking to people about money for over two decades. I've literally talked to hundreds of thousands of people through one-on-one counseling, radio show calls, live events, and a million different chance encounters. And in all that time, I've found that a lot of people's understanding of wealth is clouded by two toxic lies.

Some people believe that wealth is the answer to all of life's problems—that if they can just get rich, everything will be okay. That's the first lie. Others believe that wealth means the person holding it is evil, that they did something immoral in order to get rich. That's the second lie. Both are common in our culture, and both have caused all kinds of harm to all kinds of people.

Because of the nature of my job, I've had the pleasure of getting to know many, many wealthy families. Most of those I've spent time with are some of the best people on earth. Others, though, have had a different reaction to their wealth. Even among the ultrasuccessful, these toxic lies about wealth have made it hard to see whether or not the wealth is worth it. Some have grown guilty about their success while others have developed an arrogant, entitlement mindset about it. A question seems to loom over the whole issue of wealth: Is it a blessing or a curse?

That's something my wife, Sharon, and I have dealt with as we've raised our three children. With the youngest one in college now, we can only pray that we've done enough to pass along not just the wealth, but also the *character* to carry that wealth. It struck us early on that if we didn't pour into their character, the wealth our kids inherit will absolutely destroy their lives. That's a pretty sobering thought for any parent.

Fortunately for me, others—even those much more successful than I—have faced these same concerns. And if this book is any indication, they've already figured it out. I've always told people that if you want to win, go find some winners and do what they do. If you want to get in shape, spend some time with athletes. If you want to have a long, happy marriage, go spend time with a couple that's been married for sixty years and is still holding hands. And if you want to have a healthy respect for wealth, go find a wealthy person who's doing it right. I can't think of anyone better suited for this task than my friend Truett Cathy.

I've admired Truett for decades. His incredible faith, spiritual maturity, humility, and generous spirit—not to mention his unbelievable business success—have perfectly suited him to write this book, which I think is the most important thing he's ever written.

When someone like Truett Cathy asks the question, "Is wealth worth it?" I have no choice but to sit down and read that book. I'm glad that you've chosen to do the same.

THE POWER
OF WEALTH

The Power to Build
or to Break Down

This book is filled with caution, because wealth has the power to build up and to destroy. As much as I would prefer to write only the inspiring stories of people who have used wealth to make the world a better place, you and I have seen both sides of that coin. We see gleaming cities and broken families. The hard working and the spoiled. The joy that comes from giving generously and the jealousies that can escalate into violence.

Like wealth, poverty also has the power to build us up and make us appreciate what we have, or it can break our spirits. During the Great Depression, my father and many others buckled under the weight of the same financial hardships that gave the Greatest Generation the strength to build modern America.

I have experienced poverty and plenty, and I've decided that I much prefer living with plenty.

At the same time, I appreciate the many lessons to be learned from poverty—lessons my children and grandchildren will never experience first-hand. I can only describe to them what it was like to wonder whether the coal would run out before the winter did. They will never hear a grocer tell them they cannot buy more food because their parents have not paid what they owe on their account. My great-grandchildren may take part-time jobs when they become teenagers, and the income from those jobs will be theirs to spend, save, or give as they choose. In the 1930s, when my friends and I were young, our after-school and weekend jobs put food on our family's table. That responsibility led us to understand the power of money to literally keep us alive.

That was a long time ago, and we have since become a wealthy nation. Some days I wonder if wealth is a good thing.

.   .   .

In recent years I have enjoyed collecting classic or unusual cars when the price is right. When I had the opportunity to buy the Batmobile that appeared in the movie *Batman Returns*, I decided to display it at the Chick-fil-A home office. I wish I could show instead the first bicycle I ever bought. Nobody had much money in the 1920s, and it took me a long time selling Coca-Colas to save enough nickels to buy that four-dollar used bike from Werner McElroy. It didn't have fenders, and it needed work, but I have more pleasant memories of that bike than any automobile I ever bought, because I worked for it and I fixed it up.

Our sweetest memories are often simpler times, when our children were young and we were working hard together as a family. For my wife, Jeannette, and me, life revolved around our Dwarf House restaurant, our church, and our children's school. We lived on a farm in the country where our children's activities weren't all that different from the ones I had enjoyed as a child in the Depression: hide-and-seek, skipping rope, and playing marbles.

Of course, my childhood times in the Depression were not always sweet. My mother struggled for years to make ends meet by running a boardinghouse. When the first government-supported housing project opened in Atlanta, we moved there, believing we could make the reduced monthly rent payments from my father's small income and my brother's and my newspaper sales. We could not. Our home had to be our livelihood, not just a place to live. We had to move out of Techwood Homes and find another house that we could rent and operate as a boardinghouse. We lived there on Myrtle Street in Atlanta until my brother and I were drafted, and our parents moved to Jenkinsburg to live with our sister.

Even in those difficult times, my mother's smiles seemed to make things much better.

• • •

I once heard a story about a man who earned a hundred dollars a week, and he made a commitment to be faithful with his tithe. Every Sunday morning he happily placed a ten-dollar bill in the offering plate. Over time his responsibilities at work increased, and his pay rose along with it. He earned more money, so he and his wife bought a bigger house, and they shared special gifts with their children. He continued to tithe, but giving became more of an effort. Sometimes at the end of the week he didn't have enough left to pay his tithe, and he felt guilty. Finally, he was making a thousand dollars a week, and he just couldn't afford to put a hundred dollars in the offering every week. So he went to his pastor and asked if he could be released from the commitment he had made to tithe his earnings.

The preacher said he could not release a man from a commitment he had made with God. "What we can do instead," the preacher said, "is pray that you'll get that hundred-dollar-a-week job again so it will be easier for you to tithe."

Like the rich young ruler in the parable, the man went away sad. He had committed so much of his income to a big mortgage and car payment and satellite television, he and his wife could not give generously, even when they wanted to. They looked around at all they had accumulated and asked themselves, "Wealth, is it worth it?"

It's easy to lose sight of the things that really matter when we have all the comforts we desire.

· · ·

Working behind the counter of our Dwarf House restaurant over the years, I served thousands of meals to chief executives, line workers, and unemployed folks. I got to know families, and I watched children grow up, get married, and start their own families.

My son Dan, who is president of Chick-fil-A, likes to say we grow our business big by staying small, and by that I think he means that we should enjoy simple pleasures. We have more than fifteen hundred restaurants in the chain, but each of those restaurants represents a family creating its own sweet memories. By "staying small," we also remain sensitive to the needs of others around us.

As I began thinking about this book and asking myself the question, "Wealth, is it worth it?" three men came to mind. They are all about the age of our children, and they all became wealthy, although they all had very different circumstances growing up. One grew up in financial hardship. Though times were good in the 1950s, there are always poor among us, and this boy's family had a difficult time keeping shoes on their children's feet. But the boy was very smart, and as a young man he started his own company, becoming a millionaire many times over before his fortieth birthday.

Another of the men I knew grew up much like our children, with hard-working parents managing their own small business. Like the first, he became very wealthy, then he leveraged his assets to borrow millions more so he could grow his company even faster.

The third boy had parents who were considered by many in our community to be wealthy, and he inherited the family business.

I think about these three men today because two of them have lost their companies and the third faces bankruptcy. Two of them are divorced. These men had it all, and then they lost it all. I don't know the circumstances that led to their difficulties. I can only imagine that they lost sight of the things that really mattered to them—they didn't spend enough time counting their blessings—and now they ask themselves, "Wealth, is it worth it?"

Warren Buffett Asks, "Why Wait?"

The encouraging examples of people I have known or admired remind me of the beneficial power of wealth. At the time I am writing this, the two wealthiest men in America—Bill Gates and Warren Buffett—appear to be asking themselves if wealth is worth it, and they're coming up with an unusual response. They're giving away the largest part of their fortunes. They've decided that wealth is worth it if they put it to work doing good things in the world rather than leave it sitting in their bank accounts or their portfolios.

I've had the opportunity to become friends with Warren Buffett in recent years, and as I was putting together this book I couldn't think of anyone more qualified to answer some of my questions about wealth. He graciously agreed to spend time discussing the issues with me.

Q: *Warren, how do you define wealth?*

A: Wealth is having enough. That means to some people, no matter how much they have, they can't really be wealthy because they want more than they've got. Somebody once said that success is getting what you want; happiness is wanting what you get.

Once you can take care of yourself and your family and everything you need, beyond that it's a bunch of claim checks. If you think about money, it's a claim check on other people's products and services. When you've got enough to take care of yourself, more claim checks don't do you any good. But they can do a lot of good for all kinds of other people.

When you've got enough, you ought to start seeing that other people have enough, in my view.

Q: *You are in the process of giving away billions of dollars. What is your motivation?*

A: Giving to others has been a philosophy that my wife and I agreed on back when we were in our twenties. I felt then that I would compound money at a high rate, therefore if I focused on accumulating it for a significant period of time, there would be a huge amount of money to be used later, as opposed to giving away the money earlier. She was much more for doing it early on. We compromised on that, but when she died in 2004, I had to put a plan into motion to make sure it was given away.

I have arranged that all of the money—and it will be more than 99 percent of what I earned— will be distributed by, at the latest, ten years after my estate is settled. It won't go out for fifty or a hundred years. Who knows what people would be doing with the money then. I have people I am confident in who are distributing it now.

The money doesn't do me any good. It's just a bunch of stock certificates sitting in a safe deposit box. Those stock certificates have been down there for about forty years.

I've never given away anything I need. I've gotten everything I want and everything my family needed. I've been blessed in a million ways. Beyond that, those stock certificates can do all kinds of things for other people. They can vaccinate millions of children. They can educate children. They can do all kinds of things. They can't do anything for me other than make me feel like I have more money than somebody else. But so what? I've never given up a movie, never given up a dinner, never given up a vacation trip to give away money. I happen to have a lot more than my family and I need, and other people can use it very well.

Q: *What about your children?*
A: I do not believe in family dynasties. America was built on the idea of equality of opportunity. The idea of dynasties goes directly against that. I can build a pyramid to myself. That's what people did in Egypt. They made all kinds of people work to build them a pyramid so that a couple of thousand years later people would look at it. I don't have any inclination in that way at all.

I want my kids to live well, and they do. They are productive citizens who participate in philanthropy in a big way. Each one of the three of them spends all day working at that.

Q: *I know that you are encouraging other wealthy people to share their wealth. How is that going?*

A: We have this campaign of sorts, Bill and Melinda Gates and myself, and we've gotten fifty-nine people in the *Forbes* 400 to pledge to give away more than half of their wealth. Most of these people were going to do it anyway, but they are more committed. The commitment will increase the percentage that some people will give away.

I talked to one fellow—I had sent some material to him first—and he sent the material to his two children. These people are all very rich. So his two boys called him up and said, "Dad, do it. It makes more sense for you to give it away than pouring money onto us."

Q: *What do you tell young people who have not yet become wealthy?*

A: I had one hundred sixty college students visiting here last Friday—I do that six times a year—and I get a lot of questions on philanthropy, and I answer them just like I'm answering you. I also tell them that love is the one thing you can't give too much of. The more you try to give away, the more you get back. There is no way you can deplete your store of love. But if you don't give it out, love disappears. You can't hold on to it, or it goes away.

. . .

The lesson from Warren Buffett, then, is that for wealth to be worth it, you have to give it away. You have to let it flow through your hands and go to places where it can work. Wealth that does nothing but acquire possessions for our own enjoyment soon grows stagnant and stale.

Money and possessions for their own sake are a hollow victory. Real victory is what you do with the money, not the fact that you have it.

The truth is,
you always get back
more than you give away.
Some people never learn that.
They're busy cheating people,
cutting corners, lying to them,
all kinds of things, and they
think they're a success because
they have tens of millions of
dollars later in life. I don't
think they are a success, and I
don't think deep down they feel
like they are a success.

WARREN BUFFETT

One Man's Definition of Wealth and Its Limits

When I began to work on this book, I asked friends and acquaintances the question in the title: Wealth, is it worth it? No one responded with an unqualified yes or no. One of the most illuminating answers came from a man I met at our pizza restaurant, Upscale Pizza, in Fayetteville, Georgia. Joe Ard said that the answer depends on how you define wealth. Years ago, his father's definition of wealth was, if a man can go to sleep at night and not have to worry about how he will pay his bills, he is a wealthy man. Isn't that the truth? Burdened neither by poverty nor so much stuff that he has difficulty falling asleep—that's a wealthy man.

Then Joe reminded me of the limitations of wealth. "I have a good business, an excellent income, good friends, and a loving relationship with my heavenly Father," he said. "But I needed something wealth or money could not provide.

You see, my wife of seventeen years went to be with the Lord on July 8, 2010, after a twelve-year battle with cancer. Most people think a lot of money will fix everything. In July I lost the most important thing on this earth, and no amount of money could have stopped it."

I felt Joe's pain as he spoke, remembering the loss of my two brothers as young men in an airplane crash and the fear of my own death when I underwent surgery to remove colon cancer before my fortieth birthday. Six months after the surgery and a painful reaction to the anesthesia, I had to go back for a second surgery. As Jeannette and I left our home for the hospital, I would have given my last dime to keep from being taken from her and our three children.

Money has tremendous power for good or evil, but as Joe and I were shown, that power also has limits.

Never forget:
the secret of creating riches
for oneself is to create
them for others.

SIR JOHN TEMPLETON

Yes, If...

My pastor and best friend, Dr. Charles Q. Carter, and I discussed whether wealth is worth it, and he suggested the simplest qualifications for answering yes. I believe we can all agree on these qualifications:

- Yes, if you earn it honestly. I believe in hard work and the rewards we earn from it. A good day is one you can look back on and see your accomplishments.

- Yes, if you spend wisely and save reasonably. Many hard-working people who have earned a lot of money are financially insolvent because they overspend. Everybody needs a budget, a plan for spending and saving that allows them to buy the things they need and put enough aside for long-term requirements.

- Yes, if you give generously. This is my favorite

part of the answer. Our blessings are not meant to be held in our pockets. God wants our blessings to flow through us like a river so they can bless others.

Three simple answers, each beginning with yes. Or you can turn the answers around and ruin everything. Millions of people have. Then the answer to, Wealth, is it worth it? becomes:

- No, if you have not worked for it. I've seen easy money or too much money ruin too many lives. I've also seen families torn apart when people devote so much of their time to making money that they neglect their spouse, their children, or their health.

- No, if you spend it frivolously. Open your eyes any day of the week to see the result of overspending and overborrowing. Did you know that, according to *Sports Illustrated* magazine, 78 percent of professional football players are bankrupt two years after they retire? These young men work as hard as anybody in America, but poor investments and poor spending decisions too often cost them everything.

- No, if you don't bother to save for the future. Again, it's a matter of balance. In the United States, millions of people in my children's generation face an uncertain future because they are not saving enough to support themselves in retirement.

- No, if you are not willing to share your wealth. The happiest people I know are those who give away their money. The saddest are those who hold their possessions in their hearts instead of their hands, or who hoard because they fear what the future may bring.

Whoever loves
money never has enough;
whoever loves wealth
is never satisfied with
their income.

ECCLESIASTES 5:10, NIV

A Hunger That Destroys

I was two years old in 1923, and my father was trying desperately to earn a living by selling real estate in Eatonton, Georgia, a town just east of Atlanta. A story is told of a gathering of the world's wealthiest men that same year a world away at the Edgewater Beach Hotel in Chicago, including:

- Howard Hopson, head of one of the country's largest utilities conglomerates;
- steel titan Charles M. Schwab (not the founder of Charles Schwab & Company, the discount brokerage);
- Richard Whitney, who later became president of the New York Stock Exchange;
- Arthur Cutton, who became one of America's richest men through stock speculation;
- Leon Fraser, who later became president of the Bank for International Settlements;
- Albert Fall, U.S. Secretary of the Interior;

- Jesse Livermore, a wildly successful market speculator;
- Ivan Kreuger, owner of a huge match company that was a front for an investment pyramid scheme;
- Samuel Insull, owner of several transportation and utilities companies.

Of course, my parents were not aware of the meeting and probably would not have recognized any of the men's names. However, those men and my father had something in common: a hunger for wealth that would ultimately damage or even destroy them.

You don't have to be rich in order to be driven by a desire for money, and my father was never rich. Throughout my childhood in the 1920s and 1930s, Dad was unable to generate income for our family. He had been a successful farmer until fire destroyed the family home and he lost the farm. We moved to Atlanta in 1924, and my mother became the primary breadwinner, running a boardinghouse. We moved from house to house, nine moves in all, renting something a little cheaper or a little bigger so we might have room for one more boarder. The Great Depression only made matters worse for my father, who tried with little success to sell life insurance. The experience left him broken, if not completely broke. I rarely saw him smile and never heard him say, "I love you."

My mother, facing the same circumstances, did what it took to keep food on the table and a

No man can tell
whether he is rich or poor
by turning to his ledger.
It is the heart that makes a
man rich. He is rich according
to what he is, not according
to what he has.

HENRY WARD BEECHER

roof over our heads, usually with a smile and always with a kind word.

Years earlier, my sister Esther had polio at age two, but she never let her leg braces, crutches, or wheelchair stop her from achieving her goals. She went to college and got a job teaching, and she would send us twenty-five dollars a month from her paycheck, which couldn't have been more than a hundred dollars. We looked forward to that twenty-five dollars to help get us over the hump.

I can't explain how bad it was during the Depression; people lived in poverty and got by with what they had. No credit was available anywhere. I had to work hard to help my mother in our boardinghouse by shucking corn, shelling peas, setting the table, and washing dirty dishes.

Things were so bad that the city of Atlanta had to pay schoolteachers in scrip, which was a form of credit. Rich's Department Store would exchange cash for that scrip and hold it until the city could redeem the scrip. Richard Rich earned a lot of lifelong customers for his stores with that gesture.

If a rich man
is proud of his wealth,
he should not be praised
until it is known how
he employs it.

SOCRATES

Wealth and Real Wealth

By the time World War II began, my father had outlived the Depression, but he still carried the scars of pessimism and negativity. My mother died of acute appendicitis and finally found her rest. Of the men who had gathered at the Edgewater Beach Hotel two decades earlier, most were either broke, in prison, or dead by their own hand. Hopson was sentenced to seven years in prison for fraud and income tax evasion. He lost a $74 million fortune and died in a sanitarium. Schwab died broke in 1939, owing $1.7 million. Whitney outspent his income and turned to embezzlement, costing him a five-to-ten-year sentence in Sing Sing prison. Cutton was indicted for income tax evasion, but he died in 1937 before being brought to trial. Fraser took his own life. Fall was convicted of bribery and spent a year in prison. Livermore took his own life. Kreuger's company went under in 1932, and he took his own life.

When I heard about the lives and deaths of those wealthy, powerful men, I thought about some other people I had heard about or had known personally—men and women who gained tremendous wealth only to see it damage them or the generations they left it to. This caused me to wonder about the legacy I might be leaving.

I am a father of three, grandfather of twelve, and now a great-grandfather. The Lord and a growing group of talented men and women have blessed me with a chain of more than fifteen hundred restaurants with nearly $4 billion in annual sales. I guess by most standards that would make me wealthy. But that is not a description I am comfortable with or proud of. One time a boy asked if he could shake my hand, and as we clasped hands, he said, "Look, I'm shaking the hand of a millionaire." Suddenly I felt very self-conscious. If I'm a millionaire, then I've built a big bank account, and that's the most negative thing I can think about myself. Material wealth cannot buy honor or happiness, and a title based on the size of my assets is the last thing I desire.

One of the worst things I can imagine somebody saying about me is, "He's a rich old man." Instead, my prayer at this point is to live a worthy life and to leave a legacy similar to the one my mother left to me of hard work, loving-kindness, generosity, and respect for the power of wealth to do good or to do harm. That impact will outlive any monetary wealth I leave behind.

The story of the powerful men focuses on the negative aspects of wealth, and we should not shy from telling those stories. However, let's not dwell on them for too long. The Bible reminds us to think about things that are true, noble, just, pure, lovely, virtuous, and praiseworthy. Wealth alone is none of these things. But wealth in the hands of people who are filled with these virtues can make a powerful, positive difference in the world. People like Walt Disney, Henry Ford, and Bill Marriott. They not only created products and services that make our lives more enjoyable, but they were incredibly generous with their money.

On a much smaller scale, I think about Mr. and Mrs. Lobach. Of course you have never heard of them, but Mr. and Mrs. Lobach were rich, at least in my eyes as a boy in the 1920s. Not long after we moved to Atlanta and started taking in boarders, they knocked on our door. They both dressed professionally, and they kept a nice automobile. They had no children, and both of them had jobs at Southern Railroad. There were times in those days when I could sense my parents were low on cash. Mom might serve salmon croquettes instead of fried chicken, or the house might be colder in winter. Occasionally during one of those difficult times, we might receive a delivery of coal that I was pretty sure was more than we could afford. I believe the Lobachs were helping us out.

To give without any reward, or any notice, has a special quality of its own.

ANNE MORROW LINDBERGH

The Lobachs became our good friends, and they stayed in our boardinghouse for several years. They were the only married couple I remember who stayed with us for any length of time.

Many years later the Lobachs lived in an apartment at Christian City, a community for senior citizens in south Fulton County, Georgia. My sister Gladys, who also had a unit at Christian City, helped take care of them in their final years. It was the best way she knew to say thank you for their help years earlier.

The Lobachs and Gladys demonstrated the power of money to warm hearts by helping others. They never drew attention to themselves in their giving. Instead, they saw someone in need, and they quietly reached out and met that need.

The only question
with wealth is,
what do you do with it?

JOHN D. ROCKEFELLER

Caution: Wealth in Your Family

The headline caught my eye: "A Prominent Atlanta Family Comes Apart."

I read the article sadly, and I saw the damaging power that money can have on relationships.

I know this family. They are good, generous, and loving. Their early history is similar to my own family's, and their success was something to admire. A boy grows up on a north Georgia farm and works his way through the Great Depression. After the war he joins his brother in a partnership to build a business.

Their business became one of our city's most successful companies. It was recognized by *Forbes* magazine as the nation's number-one service company, and he was listed by *Forbes* as one of the wealthiest four hundred people in America.

Over several decades he and his wife gave many millions of dollars to colleges and universities, hospitals, schools, and children's causes. My friend passed away in 1991, and his two sons became chairman and CEO of the company that bears the family name on the New York Stock Exchange. Eighteen years later, in 2009, my friend's widow died, and in 2010 the legal action began. This private family began a very public ordeal as family members sued, fired, and divorced one another.

And as I read about this family tragedy, I thought about the wealth they had attained, and I asked myself, "Is it worth it?"

Is it worth it to amass a fortune if that fortune splits your family? Is it worth it to inherit a large estate if that wealth separates father and son?

Our young men
today are falling into a trap.
Society is telling them
material success is what's
important, but if we buy
into that idea, we can spend
a lifetime chasing that success
and never really have the
positive impact on people
that would make our lives
truly significant.

TONY DUNGY

Tony Dungy
on the Definition of Success

Tony Dungy has won a Super Bowl as a player for the Pittsburgh Steelers and as head coach of the Indianapolis Colts. Most people would say those accomplishments would establish him as a "success." But Tony's concern for the hearts and minds of young people make him the greatest success in my opinion. He believes the path to significance is not necessarily through success, as the world defines the term. I asked him to share his thoughts on success and significance, especially in the context of professional football.

Q: *Tony, you've written about "the trap of material success." What do you tell young players to keep them from falling into that trap?*
A: I tell them how I've seen so many guys come into our team and make a lot of money and leave at end of their career. You're not going to be able

to judge success on how much money you made. If you do, you'll be disappointed at the end.

So many guys say, "I did all that. I achieved. But what do I have to show for it when I'm thirty-five years old and retired? Was it worth it if that's all I get from it?"

I've seen that happen over and over again. So you start talking about relationships, putting down roots in a community and becoming part of the life of the community. Those are the things that are going to last. And the relationships you have with your children. So many of our guys have young kids when they start their careers. Now your children are ten or eleven years old, and where is that relationship going? What are you drawing from? That relationship doesn't depend on how much money you made, or whether you got that big contract. That's not going to be what you remember when it's all said and done.

Q: *Has your definition of success changed from your days as a professional football player?*

A: Success for me at that point was wrapped up in what I wanted to do. I set goals, and if I achieved that goal, I was successful. I wanted to get a college scholarship, and I got that. Therefore, it was a success. That was how I looked at things. It was all based on what I wanted to do and what my goals were, and most of it centered around me.

As you get older, and as I matured as a Christian, I realized that it doesn't have to center around me. Now I look at success more in terms of my team and other people in my community, and being able to make an impact—not just to succeed personally.

Q: *Do today's players have a different definition of success from the days when you were playing?*
A: They probably look at it the same. You start out looking at success as an individual. You look at success as: If I climb the ladder; if I make a certain amount of money; if I have achieved certain goals, then I am successful. That hasn't changed over the years. Then you grow into learning there is more to life than just personal achievement.

Q: *Is the National Football League doing anything to help those players?*

A: NFL teams in the last ten to twelve years have started doing financial education, bringing in speakers, talking to players about long-term planning. Even before we did it as an organization, I talked to the players about decision making, about planning for their future, about realizing they're not going to be at this earning level their whole life.

The earning power you are at as a professional athlete is unrealistic. To be twenty-one years old and start at the top and make half a million dollars, and think it's always going to be that way. That is what so many of our guys have problems with. Now they're thirty and they come back to a job where they're making fifty thousand a year, and they're disappointed. They think, *How can I possibly live like this?* And yet they're still living better than 90 percent of the people in the country. But they're not used to it because they had this unrealistic start. That's what so many of our people have to learn.

Q: *Are there any players modeling true significance for their teammates?*

A: More guys are demonstrating the whole idea of responsibility and giving back to the community. Some of them are also understanding that this lifestyle isn't going to go on forever. That's what young guys need to see. Unfortunately, when you're twenty-one, you think the long-term future is three years from now. To think about where you're going to be in ten years, fifteen years, what would you like to do, that's a foreign concept.

But more players are thinking about that. The NFL is doing better job of getting the statistics out and preparing the players, reminding them that, unfortunately, we still have too many former players who within four or five years of leaving the game are filing for bankruptcy or looking for aid because they've gone through a lot of money very quickly. You can do it if you're not careful.

Q: *What kind of progress are we making with boys and the dads' responsibilities in the homes?*

A: That has been one of the problems for our

players. So many of our players did not have that kind of financial training or decision-making training from their dads, because they didn't grow up with their dad. For many guys, this is new to them to talk about saving, about planning, about budgets. It starts when you're young.

Even if you have that training at twenty-one or twenty-two years old, you might not make the best decisions. Think about being handed $2 million when you're twenty-one years old, and you've never thought about budgeting, planning, or lifestyle decisions.

Q: *Finally, how do you answer the question, "Wealth, is it worth it?"*
A: I would say not always. If you get wealth before you learn how to use it, it can be a burden on you more than a blessing. But if you learn how to use it and learn how not to be fooled by it, wealth can be a very big blessing.

I'm grateful to my dad for a lot of things, but one of the things I'm most grateful for is that he taught me the value of a dollar. He taught me that you can make good decisions, and you can do just fine without being the richest person in the world. Now that I do have plenty, I'm so glad I got that training, because I'm not fooled by the trappings of money.

.   .   .

Tony is a spokesman for All Pro Dad, a program that helps men become better fathers. This work is important because when fathers are in the home taking a positive, active role, those children are much less likely to grow up in poverty. They are more likely to stay in school and out of trouble that can eventually lead to criminal behavior.

In fact, the National Fatherhood Initiative found that children in father-absent homes are five times more likely to be poor. And fatherless children are twice as likely to drop out of school, leading directly to poverty.

Growing up with involved, responsible, and committed fathers has a tremendous impact on the future financial well-being of children.

EARN
WEALTH
HONESTLY

Ten Little Words

For many years I have handed out cards with ten little, two-letter words:

IF IT IS TO BE, IT IS UP TO ME.

In these ten words lies the key to our own success in this do-it-yourself world. My pastor makes the same point in a story he tells of a man who bought twenty acres of land and worked for months with his mule to pull out stumps and clear brush. The following spring he planted his seed, and later in the summer a minister passed by and stopped to admire. The minister called over to the farmer, "Well, brother, looks like you and the Lord got yourselves a beautiful farm here."

"That's right, sir," the farmer replied, "but you should have seen it when the Lord had it by himself."

The point of the story is clear: God gives us opportunities to plow the field, but we have to plow it ourselves if we expect to make a harvest. God has created a wonderful world for us to live in, but He doesn't carve statues from the marble He made. He doesn't saw trees into lumber for houses or turn grapes into jelly. It takes hard work on our part.

J. Paul Getty, a twentieth-century oil tycoon who was at one time America's richest man, had a simple formula for making money: "Get up early. Work hard. Find oil." The first time you read that advice, "Find oil," you might think Getty was suggesting that we rely on luck. But for an oilman, finding oil isn't a matter of luck. The process begins with preparation, engineering, and a lot of hard work at drilling wells—not always successfully. The same is true in the restaurant business, banking, technology, sports, or any other worthwhile endeavor. What appears to be luck or an overnight success is built on a foundation created through many years of hard work.

Genius
is 1 percent inspiration
and 99 percent
perspiration.

THOMAS EDISON

If it takes
seven days to make a living,
you ought to be doing
something else.

STC

Working Hard and Having Fun

F rank Gordy was one of the hardest-working people I knew growing up, and yet he made his work enjoyable. In fact, it wasn't until I got into the restaurant business that I understood how hard Mr. Gordy was working every day at his Varsity Drive-In in Atlanta. He was always smiling and visiting with his customers—he made running a restaurant look easy.

I was a teenager in the 1930s, and The Varsity was already an Atlanta institution. We lived a few blocks away in Techwood Homes, Atlanta's first public housing project, and every time I walked over for one of those nickel chili dogs and a Coke, Mr. Gordy would smile and greet me as if he had been waiting all day for me to drop in. He called his restaurant "The Fun Place to Eat," and it really was.

Over time I learned more about Mr. Gordy and The Varsity. Like me, he had not considered himself to be college material. His mother did, however, and she insisted that he at least try

Georgia Tech as a freshman in 1926. After one semester he left Tech, promising his freshman classmates that he would be worth twenty thousand dollars by the time they graduated. Instead, he was worth forty thousand dollars.

In 1928, when he would have been a junior at Tech, he opened a little restaurant down the street from the Institute and sold hot dogs to the college students. As his business grew, he branched out and opened a barbershop and a pool hall with a little duckpin bowling alley in some adjacent buildings—anything to keep the Tech boys close by until they got hungry.

I was fifteen years old when we moved into Techwood Homes in 1936, and because of my success with my newspaper route, I always had a little change in my pocket. Even then I recognized the quality of the products Mr. Gordy was selling. A few years later, when I was courting, I would sometimes take my date to The Varsity, where I could spend a quarter, and we would each have a hot dog and a Coke with a nickel left over to tip the carhop. Teenagers from all over Atlanta gathered at The

Ringing the cash
register is not the name of
the game. It's only the
scorekeeper, and it's not what
motivates me. I'm motivated
in my business by the
compliments I receive about
our people, our service,
and the quality of our food.

STC

Varsity, especially on Friday and Saturday nights. Mr. Gordy always kept an eye on the parking lot, making sure everybody was having a good time and nobody was getting into trouble.

Over the years Frank Gordy became my friend and my model for operating a business successfully. Three things he did particularly stand out:

- Serve fresh, high-quality ingredients. The meat, bread, and produce trucks made deliveries to The Varsity every day—twice on busy days—and Mr. Gordy inspected every delivery. He tasted the chili every morning to make sure it had been prepared properly.

- Greet as many customers as possible. At lunchtime he often directed traffic with a smile in the parking lot.

- Make sure every customer leaves satisfied. On those days when tens of thousands streamed through The Varsity, quick service became a higher priority. We customers were happy to do our part, stepping up to the counter with our money in our hand and our order on our mind. Speed actually became part of the fun of the place.

Love what you do,
and you'll never work
a day in your life.

STC

Grace and Hard Work

F rank Gordy always assumed his son, Frank Jr., would take over The Varsity, but Frank Jr. died unexpectedly in 1980. Mr. Gordy died three years later, and his daughter, Nancy, was faced with either helping her mother sell The Varsity or running it herself.

Nancy had never worked behind the counter and had never managed employees. As it turned out, however, Nancy combined her father's hard-work ethic and her mother's grace to manage The Varsity very successfully. Nearly thirty years later, thousands still stream through every day, with Nancy greeting many of them personally in front of the counter. It's a treat for me to sit down with a chili dog that tastes as delicious as my first one nearly eighty years ago.

Nancy is now in the process of turning over The Varsity to her children, who understand that their relationship with this important Atlanta land-mark is not one of ownership but stewardship. The most important thing Frank Gordy did to ensure a permanent place for The Varsity was to give his customers the idea that *they* own the place, not the Gordy family. So, today, the third generation stands in the midst of the lunchtime crowd that lines up at that long, long counter, listening to the echoes of "What'll you have! What'll you have!" through the dining room and the years.

Everybody
likes to be a winner,
whether you're playing
checkers or you're in business.
You like to be competitive,
so you figure out how you can
do what you do better than
your competition.

STC

The Winning Edge

My friend Rick Johnson, who directed our WinShape Camps for twenty-five years, once told me about waking up at three o'clock in the morning to the bouncing of a basketball out in the driveway. Rick got out of bed and went outside to find his teenage son, Brad, shooting baskets. Rick wondered what in the world Brad was doing playing basketball at that time of the night, and Brad explained that he was getting an edge on his opponents. None of them would be practicing in the middle of the night.

Brad's hard work served him in both basketball and football, where he played quarterback. He was a high school All-American in both sports. Florida State University offered him a scholarship, and he played football and basketball as a freshman, starting eleven basketball games. But to be successful, a major college quarterback needs to focus his attention on football year-round, so Brad gave up basketball.

His dedication and hard work at Florida State earned Brad tremendous respect, and even though he was not a starter in his senior year, he was drafted by the Minnesota Vikings and given a chance in the National Football League. He made the most of his opportunity, turning it into a seventeen-year career with the Vikings, the Tampa Bay Buccaneers, and the Dallas Cowboys. Brad was one of the most accurate passers in the league—the only quarterback in history to complete more than 60 percent of his passes in ten consecutive seasons.

I had a satellite dish installed at our house so I could watch more of his games, and each time I saw him, I thought of what his dad had told me about Brad's work ethic and his commitment to being his best. He obviously never lost that drive, because Brian Billick, Brad's offensive coordinator at Minnesota, said of him, "The depth of the man and the drive to succeed borders on obsessive."

Brad's hard work and will to win took him to the very top—the dream of millions of young men—when he led the Tampa Bay Buccaneers to a 48–21 Super Bowl victory over the Oakland Raiders in 2003.

We do our best work
when the leader is nearby.
A leader who thinks,
"They're well trained;
they don't need my presence,"
is wrong. The chief needs to
be seen. When I go into a
restaurant and see that nobody
is in charge, I'm reluctant to
stay and eat. I want to see
somebody who's in charge,
making sure everything
is in good order.

STC

Ɒurnout

I don't understand the concept of burnout. It sounds like something you experience when you do too much too fast, but in most cases the opposite seems to be true. One of our more successful franchised Chick-fil-A restaurant operators surprised me with the news that he was leaving the chain.

"Why would you quit now?" I asked. "You have two restaurants, you've been with us for years, and you're doing very well."

"I just got burned out," he said.

I found that to be an odd answer, and he had a hard time explaining further, so I asked, "How many hours are you spending in your restaurants?"

"To be honest," he said, "only about four hours a day."

Suddenly the answer was clear. This operator had been one of the strongest leaders in our chain. He had built a team that could run the restaurant successfully even when he was not there. With prosperity came the idea that he could spend more and more time away, and he began to lose his connection to his restaurant, his team, and his customers.

Our personal reward and satisfaction come from knowing that we've had a productive day. When we don't make every day productive, we begin to feel like we're wasting our time, and negative thoughts creep in, leading to burnout.

At ninety, I have turned over most of the day-to-day responsibilities of running Chick-fil-A to my son Dan as president. But I cannot imagine sitting at home and watching television, waiting for "death do us part." If that's the definition of retirement, I'm not interested. So I come to the office every day I'm in town, and I travel to speaking engagements, sometimes across the country. And in a market that is financially depressed as I write, I enjoy looking for opportunities to buy undervalued real estate.

In fact, some of my most productive years have come since I passed sixty-three, the age at which many Americans retire. We have opened more than one thousand restaurants since I hit the so-called retirement age. We didn't open our first stand-alone restaurant until I was sixty-five, and now we have built nearly one thousand of them. Jeannette and I also created the WinShape Foundation the year I turned sixty-three, and today through WinShape we operate summer camps, foster homes for children, college programs, a marriage retreat center, and much, much more. My WinShape experiences are among my most enjoyable and satisfying, especially my time spent with our foster grandchildren and at summer camp.

Jeannette and I learned about Berry College and its founder, Martha Berry, about thirty years ago, and we were inspired to create the WinShape Foundation, with the simple goal of helping to shape winners. In partnership with the college, we created a program to provide WinShape scholarships. WinShape grew to include foster homes, summer camps, a retreat center, and a marriage program on the Berry campus. I never met Martha Berry, who died in 1942, but I like to think that our WinShape Foundation lives up to her motto: "Not to be ministered unto, but to minister." Ministering to others may be the ultimate example of hard work, and it is the key to success in the restaurant business or almost any other endeavor.

I missed out on what my friend calls burnout by remaining active every day and not sitting on the beach, waiting for the sunset. I have no reason to retire. I can't do a lot of things I used to do: bowling, skiing, and other activities. That's frustrating to me, now that I have time and money to do the things I like. But I gain great satisfaction by coming to the office every day and greeting people. It seems that a lot of people who visit our home office want to meet me, and I enjoy that. Nobody else can be Truett Cathy.

In most cases
we perform better when we're
busy than when we're not busy.
When we're slow, our mind
wanders. We're not as
attentive to our business.
When we're on the firing line,
we're sharper. We move more
quickly and get the job
done right.

STC

The Ministry of Hard Work

I like to see young people working hard. That's when they learn the value of a dollar and experience the reward that comes from doing a job right, especially when they are working to serve others.

High school or college students who work part-time jobs after school learn to be responsible with their paychecks because they remember how much work they put into earning it. They learn that there's no substitute for hard work. Intelligence and talent help, but hard work and dedication matter even more. And they feel the joy that comes when others compliment them for their hard work.

Most people learn the value of hard work through their jobs, but several colleges around the country teach the importance of hard work. In addition to Berry College, College of the Ozarks in southern Missouri and Alice Lloyd College in eastern Kentucky are fine examples of "work colleges" that were founded for the purpose of allowing students to earn their tuition by working on campus.

It's hard for some people to imagine today, but just a few generations ago in this country, there were many rural areas where poor young people had little opportunity to get an education. The mission of work schools was to offer an education to young people who might otherwise never even learn to read. The schools were self-sustaining, with students working on the farm or in the kitchen or the laundry to earn their way.

Years ago *The Wall Street Journal* called the College of the Ozarks "Hard Work U," and the nickname stuck. Students there earn their college education by working part-time jobs during the semester, and many earn their room and board by working full time during the summer. No federal or state loans are made, so instead of graduating with a student loan debt of $22,000, which is the national average according to *U.S. News and World Report*, College of the Ozarks graduates begin their careers debt free. That's a great reward for their hard work.

The president of College of the Ozarks, Jerry C. Davis, previously served as president of Alice Lloyd College and is a high school graduate of the Berry

Academy. Jerry has seen the power of hard work in the lives of thousands of young people, and he has also experienced that power himself. Several years ago he wrote an article for *Guideposts* magazine in which he told of running away after being kicked out of college. Eventually he had run as far as his money would take him, and he stopped in Kentucky to call home to his grandfather. Instead of telling him to come back home or to go back to school, his grandfather suggested that Jerry stay in Kentucky and find a job—to go to work. Jerry wrote in *Guideposts*:

I finally stopped fighting the world and opened up to it, asking for and accepting help from the people God placed in my path. That was the beginning of a long road that led to graduate school and a Ph.D.

Jerry became a hard-working young man serving others rather than seeking to be served, and he was transformed. Now he helps other young people in their transformation.

Yes, wealth is worth it when you earn it honestly by working hard and serving others.

When I was
a young man I observed
that nine out of ten
things I did were failures.
I didn't want to be a failure,
so I did ten times
more work.

GEORGE BERNARD SHAW

Finding Balance

How do you balance life and business? There have been times when I had to make a decision and my family had to suffer for my absence, and at other times my business has suffered because my family needed me. You balance it out, and you remember What's Important Now—WIN.

Ask yourself if financial success is worth losing your health, your spouse, or the respect of your children.

When my brother and I opened the Dwarf House restaurant, we worked alternating twelve-hour shifts for six days a week. I rented a room in a house next door and would sometimes wake in the middle of the night to help when I heard tires crunching the gravel parking lot. Once, when the grill man didn't show up, I worked thirty-six hours straight.

I enjoyed my work. I don't think I could have succeeded if I had been working that long and hard just for the money.

I also knew that the schedule I was keeping was temporary. I was single, and getting the restaurant started was my primary responsibility. By the time Jeannette and I married, I had built the business to the place where others were sharing the responsibilities. I still spent many hours in the restaurant, but I also made time to build a marriage with Jeannette that has lasted more than sixty years.

One Customer at a Time

Hard work can make up for a lot of other deficiencies. Norman "Red" Witten was nineteen years old and had been working in a Chick-fil-A restaurant for a little over a year when we offered him the opportunity to have his own store. It was 1975, when all of our restaurants were in shopping malls. Food courts had not yet been introduced, and at this particular Chesapeake Bay–area mall, our restaurant was not in the high-traffic area.

When Red took over, the store was grossing about nine thousand dollars per month in sales and had never made a profit. It was one of the lowest volume restaurants in the chain.

"I was too young to understand that failure was an option," Red says today, "so I dug in my heels and went to work. We had four employees and myself running the business, and I was working eighty hours a week. When your volume is that low, you don't have a choice except to become part of the workforce."

At the end of the first month Red counted everything up. The restaurant had made its first profit, "$321 and some change," he reported.

Red continued "living at the restaurant," as he describes it, and he and his team increased volume every month, so that by the end of his first year he had doubled his sales volume. Of course, he didn't spend every minute behind the counter. He also introduced himself to managers and employers of stores throughout the mall and invited them to eat at Chick-fil-A. We call that becoming "the mayor of the mall."

"We built the business one customer at a time," Red says. "We got a new customer, treated them right, kept them, then got another one. With the increased volume we were able to hire more people and cut back on my own hours. I couldn't keep up that pace forever. It wasn't healthy."

The following year Red increased sales by another 50 percent, and the third year, despite losing the anchor tenant at his end of the mall, he grew sales another 38 percent. Red succeeded where others had failed because he had a tremendous amount of "want to." That's a rare ingredient in people, but it's the ingredient that makes all the difference between success and failure.

Thirty-five years later, Red says that operating his stand-alone Chick-fil-A restaurant in Hampton, Virginia, is much more complicated. "It still takes a lot of hard work," he says. "Today the work is more about building teams and leadership—different from 1975, but still hard work."

A Job Well Done, No Matter How Small

Preston Root didn't have to work. In 1913 his great-grandfather's glass company won Coca-Cola's national design competition for a unique bottle. Coke bottlers had been concerned that Coke's straight-sided bottles looked like all their imitators' bottles, and they wanted a unique design. The Root Glass Company offered the contour bottle, which is recognized across the world (even in the dark) as a Coke bottle. The Root Glass Company patented and licensed the design and earned a nickel for every gross that was manufactured. Chapman J. Root became the wealthiest man in Indiana.

Later the Root family invested in Coca-Cola bottling operations, becoming one of the world's largest bottlers. Preston grew up on Florida's Space Coast in the 1960s. His story, he tells me, is one of work, reward, and the passion to make a difference.

"My father's father was killed in a plane crash when Dad was just seven years old, so by necessity my father was an independent thinker who was nurtured by his grandfather," Preston says. "Then my father was just twenty-four years old when his grandfather died in 1945 and left him the family business and all the expectations of success.

"Our family business was to become one of America's largest bottlers of Coca-Cola. As a result, my life was filled with a proud heritage of many successes. Never would money be in need for the basics of living. We were wealthy, something I didn't realize until I was in my late teens."

Despite his family's wealth, Preston remembers daily life following normal rhythms. "Dad went to work every day and came home at night," he says. He also remembers his father showing Preston and his siblings the importance of doing a job well.

"A small example of that," Preston says, "was when I was fifteen. My father stopped by after his work one day to check on how I was doing, working at a food warehouse. He quietly asked around if I was doing a good job at stocking shelves, sweeping floors, and emptying trash. He was told that I did a pretty good job, and he left satisfied that I was applying myself.

"Afterward, he told me a story I have never forgotten. He said that unless someone swept the floors well every day, the business would shut down. 'One rat in that warehouse,' he said, 'and they close their doors. Whatever you do, it has to be done well. You'll never run the place if you don't know how to sweep those floors.' It taught me a great lesson on applying myself at work."

His father also taught him the joy of working at a job you love, and Preston followed that advice. He loved the radio—listening to reports of the Apollo missions and automobile races. He even carried a transistor radio to school in his lunch box. Radio became a fun challenge. He got a job as a newsreader and then honed the craft of telling a story over the air. He had loved listening to the Indy 500 on the radio as a boy, and he jumped at the opportunity to do play-by-play radio broadcasts of automobile racing. That was more than twenty-five years ago. You can still hear Preston announcing the action live from those seventeen-second pit stops on the Motor Racing Network, which is "the voice of NASCAR."

"I was given the opportunity to bring an exciting time to someone who might not have been able to see the race that day," Preston says. "That allowed me to help make their day a little better."

Money never
made a man happy yet,
nor will it. There is nothing
in its nature to produce
happiness. The more a
man has, the more he wants.
Instead of its filling a vacuum,
it makes one.

BENJAMIN FRANKLIN

Cheaper and Faster

When you're looking for the best way to earn money, the cheaper, faster, or easier method isn't necessarily better, especially if you sacrifice quality. Two of our competitors demonstrated that truth in the 1980s when one of them offered its version of chicken nuggets. Another competitor pointed out in a humorous commercial that instead of using whole, boneless chicken breasts to make the product, the first company was using processed parts.

"What parts?" a customer in the commercial asked.

"Parts is parts," replied the man behind the counter.

The famous line became part of our culture, and a reminder that, when it comes to food, people prefer fresh ingredients to mass production.

If you're excited
about what you're doing,
it's a lot more likely that your
employees will also be excited.
People want to work for
a person, not a company.
It's about relationships.

STC

Leading by Listening

Jimmy Collins, the first executive I hired at Chick-fil-A, often said, "If you aren't selling chicken, you'd better be supporting somebody who is." In our home office we have hundreds of employees who don't sell chicken directly to guests, so every day we want to support those operators and their teams who do.

We try to be aware of the potential "ivory tower effect" that can make the home office personnel less understanding of the issues that operators and their team members face in their restaurants. All full-time employees at our home office work at least one day a year behind the counter in a restaurant, and key field people get even more in-store experience.

My son Dan, who is president and chief operating officer, spends more time in Chick-fil-A restaurants than he does in the office. Dan makes a conscious effort to lead by listening to the people who serve chicken sandwiches every day. He travels around the country each week, visiting restaurants and meeting customers, operators, and team members. Dan even camps out with Chick-fil-A customers at our restaurant grand openings. Sleeping in his tent in the parking lot alongside more than a hundred Chick-fil-A fans gives him opportunities to know our customers much better. Then he comes home with long lists of ideas for improving our system.

I met the owners of an orange grove who had lost almost everything their father had left for them and were selling the last bit of real estate at a deep discount. The son summed up his life in a single sentence: "Our father taught us how to spend money, but he never taught us how to make money."

STC

SPEND WEALTH
WISELY AND SAVE
IT REASONABLY

$\mathcal{M}$anaging $\mathcal{R}$isk

While I was traveling through the mountains of Colorado with Jeannette, we rounded a bend and saw rescue trucks and cars lined up on the side of the road. A cable stretched from one mountain to another, and we stopped for a closer look. Rescuers were bringing someone across on the cable, and from our vantage point I could not tell if there was any life in the victim.

Then I overheard one of the rescuers tell another bystander, "He wasn't wearing the right shoes, and he didn't even have a safety rope on."

The tragic situation was a real-life reminder of the message on a poster hanging on the wall in my office. Our daughter, Trudy, gave the poster to me when she was a teenager, and it shows a mountain climber with ropes and safety equipment nearing the peak, with the words, "No goal is too high if we climb with care and confidence."

Those words have served as my daily reminder to make wise choices and avoid unnecessary risks.

We can't avoid all risk, or we wouldn't get out of bed in the morning. But we can manage risk with preparation and forethought, the lack of which may have cost the life of the climber we saw, allowing a loose stone or a little slip to turn into a tragedy.

In their desire to generate more wealth—to reach what they hope will be their financial summit—too many people take on too much risk. Instead of saving money to create wealth, they borrow money to create the appearance of wealth. Or companies, in an attempt to grow bigger faster, borrow more money than they can manage.

A better path to wealth is wise spending and reasonable saving.

*Life is determined
by the decisions we make.
How we handle difficult
situations makes all
the difference.*

STC

Risk and Opportunity

I n business, debt equals risk. And debt that is not secured by assets is an even greater risk. "Leverage," they call it. In simple terms, you might buy a $100 investment by paying $10 down and borrowing $90. If the value of the investment rises 10 percent, to $110, you've doubled your equity from $10 to $20. That kind of math is very attractive. But what if the value drops 10 percent to $90? Just like that, you're wiped out. You owe $90 on an asset worth $90, and your $10 down payment is gone.

Many businesspeople use debt to grow their companies. I have borrowed money several times through the years, though nothing approaching the example above, and I remember every trip to the bank and how uncomfortable I felt until each obligation was repaid. In 1946 my brother and I borrowed $6,600 and added $4,000 of our own money to build and open the Dwarf Grill. I limited my income—I was single at the time—and I poured all my efforts into the business to quickly pay off the note. Ben died in an airplane crash three years later. When I opened my second restaurant in 1951, cash flow allowed me to expand without taking out another loan. However, in 1960, when that restaurant burned down, I was underinsured and had to borrow $90,000 to rebuild a new-concept, fast-food restaurant.

The first day the new Dwarf House opened in 1961, my customers, who were my friends, told me that they weren't ready for fast-food self-service. It was the worst day of my career. The idea of dissatisfied customers was stressful to me, yet the new restaurant was not designed to deliver traditional service with waitresses. I felt trapped. Then my friend Ted Davis took a long-term lease on the building and put Atlanta's first Kentucky Fried Chicken restaurant in the space, and I paid off my bank loan.

Relieved of the financial burden, but with only one restaurant, I spent more time with my customers, and I began to ask myself, "What else is there for Truett Cathy to do?" I had created a product we called a chicken steak sandwich, and the additional time gave me the opportunity to promote the product, which would become the Chick-fil-A chicken sandwich. Out of misfortune came opportunity.

Life Isn't Fair

Paul Harvey once told a graduating class, "You might think life is not fair. Get used to it."

I do not understand why my two brothers, who were married and had young children, both had to die in an airplane crash. The first thing I asked when I heard the news was, "God, why did this have to happen?" If God is the ruler of everything, couldn't He have prevented that crash? Couldn't He have protected my brothers and their young families?

Some situations are out of our control and beyond my understanding. That's where our faith comes in, and we have to trust the Lord. God promises that all things work together for good for those who love the Lord. That means the good and the bad. All things.

All Things
Can Work Together for Good

We opened the first Chick-fil-A restaurant in 1967 and paid for the build-out and equipment from our savings. The fact that our first restaurants were in enclosed shopping malls kept our capital outlay much lower than if we had bought real estate and built stand-alone restaurants. In fact, our financial model allowed us to open fourteen Chick-fil-A restaurants in mall locations before I finally had to go to a bank and borrow money to finance the opening of fourteen more in a single year, doubling our size.

The biggest financial crisis I ever faced came in the early 1980s, when we borrowed $10 million to build our home office building. Interest rates were pushing 20 percent, and we experienced the only year-to-year drop in same-store sales in the history of our chain. There were days when I could not see a way through that situation.

I finally experienced peace when the Chick-fil-A executive committee scheduled a retreat to address our financial problems. However, instead of addressing the business issues directly, we spent the entire time developing a statement that became our corporate purpose: "To glorify God by being a faithful steward of all that is entrusted to us. To have a positive influence on all who come in contact with Chick-fil-A."

There was no magic in the words. We did come away, however, with a commitment to focus on God and on other people first. And I was determined to never face another financial crisis. The next year sales increased 36 percent across the chain, and God opened opportunities to serve others through the creation of the WinShape Foundation.

Looking back on more than sixty years in the restaurant business, I see that what sometimes appears to be the worst situation turns out to be the best. Challenges really do become opportunities. I don't think I would have been motivated to develop and market the Chick-fil-A chicken sandwich if I had held on to two restaurants. And we might not have created our corporate purpose if we had not faced the financial difficulties of the early 1980s.

So while I would never wish for the financial difficulties I experienced anymore than I would wish to grow up in poverty, I believe these experiences worked together for the ultimate good.

When our children
were coming along, we shared
our financial and business
problems with them.
Some families avoid sharing
that information. They think
there is no need to burden
their children with business
problems. But they need to
know when we're under
pressure. When they expect
the extras in life, they need to
know we're having difficulty
making ends meet.

STC

Eliminating Long-Term Debt

We opened our first restaurant outside of a mall in 1986, and over the next twenty-five years we built and opened nearly one thousand more. Buying real estate and building restaurants required much more capital than opening restaurants in malls, but the stand-alone restaurants also generated more sales. We went back to the bank to finance our growth, which we managed at a steady pace.

Then in 2000, the first year we exceeded $1 billion in sales, we made a commitment to eliminate all of our long-term debt. We knew this decision would force us to open fewer restaurants and grow more slowly. But as I write this book, our company has almost reached our goal of being completely debt free. We scaled back our growth slightly over a ten-year period and have maintained an appropriate rate of expansion.

I prefer to grow only as fast as our cash flow allows. That way we avoid the risk of overborrowing, and we digest growth as we go. I find satisfaction by moving from one plateau to another and making sure we're doing everything right before we move on. I don't want to experience another financial endurance test. I've said many times that I can deal with just about any problem you can give me, except a financial problem.

The Lesson of the Tortoise

Some of our executives at Chick-fil-A enjoy telling the following story of our steady growth from the 1990s.

Boston Chicken was just coming onto the market with eight or nine restaurants in the Northeast. The founders served high-quality, home-style food fast, using recipes from their grandmothers. The concept was a huge hit from the outset, and by 1990 the chain had thirteen restaurants, and fifteen more by 1991. The industry watched with interest as growth continued, and in 1993 Boston Chicken made an initial public offering for $20 per share. By the end of the first day of trading the price had risen to $48.50. Now the whole world was watching Boston Chicken. They were the latest Wall Street darling.

With $51.5 million raised from the IPO, Boston Chicken leadership was talking about growing into a $1 billion company by the year 2000. That kind of talk made some of our executives nervous. Our direct competition up to that point had been fast-food hamburger restaurants plus KFC and Church's. Now, for the first time, an upscale chicken restaurant was entering the market, and they were talking about how big they were going to get. At their proposed rate of growth, they would surpass us within a couple of years. Maybe sooner.

We weighed our options. My son Dan traveled to New York to talk with some bankers about borrowing money to finance growth. A group of us met one day, and the team discussed ways to grow bigger. We needed to grow, they said, if we were going to fend off this looming threat. After what seemed like hours of discussion, I grew uncomfortable with all the talk of growth. I was not so concerned about getting bigger as I was with getting better. "If we get better," I said, "customers will demand that we get bigger."

Oftentimes businesspeople get excited by their success or their potential, and they borrow money to expand into areas in which they have no business going. They see sales and profit numbers going up and up, so they borrow more money and spread themselves thinner to take advantage of a "once-in-a-lifetime opportunity." In the blink of an eye, and without solid financial footing, a small slipup turns into a damaging or fatal fall.

The conversation then shifted to how we were going to get better, and we brainstormed ways to improve our service and our products, and we built on those ideas.

David Salyers, one of our executives, picks up the story: "Now fast-forward to the year 2000. Boston Market (same company, new name) was in bankruptcy, and Chick-fil-A hit $1 billion in sales. We had walked into that room with our focus on money instead of on our mission. Truett brought us back to our mission of serving customers better."

*Opportunity presents
itself sometimes in unusual
situations. What you think is
the worst thing turns out to
be a good thing. Difficult
circumstances challenge people
to do things they didn't know
they could do, and in those
times when the outlook
appears the worst, we find
new reasons for optimism.*

STC

ᒪong-Term Thinking

Too many companies, especially publicly traded companies, have a short-term mentality. They're always looking toward the next ninety-day report. As a private company with a long-term mentality, we make investments with an eye toward ten years down the road, not ten weeks. Surprisingly to some people, our long-term mentality delivers short-term results. As I write this book, our nation is experiencing its worst recession since I was a child. While many companies are making dramatic changes in response to the sour economy, we've just invested $6 million in an effort to take our customer service to a new level. The full impact of that investment won't be evident for years, and yet we are experiencing an immediate positive impact on sales.

We do sometimes sacrifice short-term results. We could have kept that $6 million in the bank and improved our bottom line. In the 1990s, as we watched Boston Market grow so quickly, we made the choice to forgo the opportunity to grow faster and add more money to the bottom line. We could have borrowed money and built a lot of restaurants, but we would have run into some of the same problems that Boston Market encountered. The problem with opening so many locations so fast is that it stretches you beyond your ability to identify and select leadership. So we chose to be the tortoise in that race, and for several years we picked up magazines with Boston Market on the cover. They looked much better in the short run. In the end, however, that growth didn't work out so well for them.

Don't sacrifice

quality for price. Sometimes
you have to pay more to get
something a little better, and in
the long run it's a wise
decision. When we buy real
estate for restaurants, brokers
often tell us they have a great
location where there is no competition. But we'd rather pay a
little more to be where people
are already congregated—
where the action is. You want a
restaurant to get as much
exposure as possible.

STC

Private Versus Public

The main difference between a private and a public company, in my opinion, is this: A public company is more interested in the bottom line and meeting the quarterly expectations of investors. A private company is more concerned with its people and considers the long-term impact of its decisions.

I have a personal interest in every person who comes to work for us. They know they have a job, and we're not going to take that job away to meet some short-term financial demand. We're not going to make irrational decisions or get into a business we don't know or expand beyond our comfort zone.

Even Churches Can Borrow and Build Too Much

S ome churches experience financial difficulties when they take on too much debt. I was disappointed in 2010 to read that a prominent California church had filed for Chapter 11 bankruptcy protection. The church had built a beautiful welcoming center, and then donations had fallen off, and the congregation was left owing $40 million. Seven years later the church still owed $36 million on its mortgage, along with $7.5 million to other creditors, according to an article in *The New York Times*.

As it turns out, *The Wall Street Journal* reports that more than two hundred churches filed for bankruptcy between 2008 and 2010. This is a tiny number compared with how many churches are in America, but it is troubling to learn that some church leaders can put their ministries at stake by borrowing too much money.

Buy a new house
or a new car, and you
experience circumstantial
happiness. You get a high off
the new thing, but then it loses
its shine, and you go after the
next shiny new thing.

STC

Why Keep Growing?

Some might look at the size of our business today and wonder why we would grow at all. After all, how big does a company need to be? I might be happy to maintain the status quo.

But we need to grow in order to create opportunities for our people. We grow so that others can remain confident in the future of our chain. We grow because quality people are attracted to growing companies. We will continue to grow moderately and confidently.

You're probably familiar with the parable of the talents. Before a man goes on a journey, he entrusts some of his holdings to some servants. By the time the man returns, two of the servants have worked to double his money. The third buries the money in fear. The man holds his servants accountable, giving the first two additional responsibilities and casting out the third.

The message is clear: God expects us to grow—to use our abilities to multiply the resources He has given us.

In the food business,
it only takes one mistake, one
rude team member, or one bad
sandwich to lose a customer.
Do things right each and every
time, making sure customers
get what they expect, and
sometimes more.

STC

The Worst Investment of All

I t breaks my heart to see people stand in line to buy lottery tickets, especially when so many of them look like they need to be using that money for the essentials of life. They're chasing a dream instead of working hard and saving. In many cases, the winners turn out to be the biggest losers of all.

One of the saddest lottery winner stories I have heard was about a grandfather who won $314 million in a Christmas Day lottery, and on Christmas Eve two years later he buried his grand-daughter, who had died of a drug overdose. The television show *20/20* interviewed the winner, who said that when he received his winnings, he immediately started receiving requests for finan-cial assistance—thousands of letters. He respond-ed generously, giving away more than $50 million to build churches and houses and to pay for cars. He became a real-life Santa Claus.

The love of his life was his seventeen-year-old granddaughter, and he wanted to share his joy with her. So he gave her four cars and lots of money—two thousand dollars a week—and it wasn't long before a new group of friends was attracted to her. All the grandfather wanted to do was to make his granddaughter happy. Instead, she started using all that money to buy drugs for her friends and herself.

She quickly spiraled downward, and at one point she told her grandfather she didn't care about the cars or the money or anything she might inherit. "Pawpaw," she told him, "all I care about is drugs."

Her boyfriend died of a drug overdose, and a year later she was dead too. The lottery winner told 20/20, "Since I won the lottery, I think there is no control for greed. I think if you have something, there's always someone else that wants it. I wish I'd torn that ticket up."

Isn't that always the way? How many stories do you hear of mega-million-dollar lottery winners living happily ever after? What we hear instead are stories of divorce, lawsuits, and shattered friendships.

The closest I ever came to knowing a lottery

winner personally was a young man in Florida who found more than a million dollars' worth of jewelry. When the owner could not be found, Eric was allowed to keep it. I read about Eric in the newspaper and reached out to him. Then I watched as this instant millionaire became an ATM for his friends. When the money ran out, his friends disappeared. Today Eric is a broken man who says he wishes he had never found the jewelry.

I can only remember buying two new automobiles in my life. I prefer to find a good deal on a second-hand one with twenty thousand miles on it that someone has taken good care of.

STC

A New Generation of Smart Shoppers

Jeannette came home from a shopping trip with one of our teenage grandsons, who had seen a shirt he liked but did not buy. Jeannette offered to buy the shirt for him, but he wouldn't let her do it because it was full price. He went to a store clerk, who confirmed the price of the shirt could not be marked down, then he even went to the manager.

"It's just a shirt," Jeannette said. "I'll get it for you."

But he refused.

Two weeks later he walked in our back door smiling. "Grandmama, I got that shirt for five dollars cheaper," he said.

Later Jeannette confided, "He's been hanging around his granddaddy. He knows how it works!"

I like to buy my own clothes on sale. Through the years I also enjoyed taking my foster grandchildren shopping at discount department stores for clothes and the things they need. I learned that girls are particular about the things they wear. Sometimes boys are too. One afternoon I was shopping with one of our foster grandsons at Lenox Square, one of Atlanta's nicest malls. He said that he couldn't find anything that suited him and suggested we go across the street to Phipps Plaza, with even higher fashions and an Abercrombie store.

We went home.

Economy
is half the battle of life;
it is not so hard to earn money
as to spend it well.

CHARLES H. SPURGEON

Money can
become addictive, like power.
You get a little bit and
you want just a little more.
A friend who is a developer
told me that wealth means
having just one more
piece of property.

STC

Building Capital in Real Estate

I don't invest in the stock market. I do invest in real estate. The old saying, "God isn't making any more of it," is true. So if you can find the right opportunity to buy when people are selling and the opportunity to sell when they're buying, and if you can stay patient during the short-term price swings, you'll be rewarded down the road.

When my brother and I built the Dwarf Grill in 1946, we bought a piece of property. It would have been less expensive in the short run to lease the land, but now, after more than sixty years in the same location, it's hard to imagine how much rent I would have paid.

In the 1950s I took advantage of real estate investment opportunities, buying several rental houses within a few miles of our restaurant. However, I was not as successful as a landlord as others I have known. More than once I had tenants get behind on their rent and then move out before I collected. Still, I was happy with the growing value of the property.

Then our biggest neighbor, the Atlanta airport, began to expand, opening a new terminal in 1961 and buying up property for expansion. Delta and Eastern airlines also expanded their operations, buying real estate to do so. Over a period of several years, I sold the houses I had bought and earned a nice profit. Those properties are now a small part of the nearly five thousand acres that make up Hartsfield-Jackson International Airport.

For the first twenty years of Chick-fil-A, owning the real estate underneath the restaurants was not an option. We were opening all of our restaurants in enclosed shopping malls and leasing the space from the mall operator. The only real assets on our balance sheet were leasehold improvements.

In the 1980s, when we were thinking about opening Chick-fil-A restaurants outside of shopping malls, we had a choice of either buying or leasing real estate. Just like it was in 1946, leasing would have been less expensive in the short run, and our short-term profits would have been greater. But we're not in business for the short run.

We want to experience the long-term advantages that ownership provides, especially growth in value and the ability to control what happens to the property. It is always our strong preference to buy. The only exception is when the best sites are not for sale, then we lease.

Buying land for hundreds of new restaurants required long-term bank financing for the real estate and the building shell. We didn't borrow for the equipment and furnishings, however. We paid for them out of cash flow, just as we had been doing throughout the years when we built restaurants in malls. That conservative approach kept us from overextending ourselves with our borrowing.

The Lord
only gives us twenty-four
hours a day to enjoy the
blessings he's given us.
Maybe someday he'll double
that and give us more time to
enjoy life even more.

STC

The Impossible Dream

I call it our *Impossible Dream*. It's a penthouse condominium in New Smyrna Beach, Florida, and it's beyond anything I ever imagined. The original owner had it designed like a ship, with teakwood everywhere and no square corners, even on the custom-made furniture. Windows open to the east, where we can watch the sunrise from the Atlantic Ocean, and the west, where we watch it set over the river and marshes. There can't be a more beautiful place than that.

I have lived my life by taking advantage of unexpected opportunities, and the *Impossible Dream* is another one. It had been listed for sale at a price much higher than we would have considered paying for it, but the months dragged on and the price kept dropping until it was available for close to a third of the original price.

Over time the economy will recover, and we'll enjoy a nice return on our investment. You might wonder why a ninety-year-old man is making long-term investments. Well, I don't plan to leave anytime soon. In the meantime, Jeannette and I are enjoying our *Impossible Dream*.

I look around and see a lot of people in their forties and fifties buying things we're just now buying in our eighties and nineties. That was not the opportunity we were given. I was forty-six years old when we opened our first Chick-fil-A restaurant, and we devoted our time and resources to building the company. When I was sixty, we built a $10-million home office. We had to borrow a lot of money to do it, and interest rates were high. That was not a time to be spending any money unnecessarily.

Now that we are in a position to buy and invest in things outside the company, I have to be careful not to let my ego grow too big. You know what ego stands for: Edging God Out!

Wealth can change the characteristics of an individual if he's not careful. It causes him to mix with a different crowd and to forget about what's important. He's achieved some worthy goals, and he slows down to enjoy them. And if we gaze too long at the sunset, we might not get up from the chair.

Poverty oftentimes can be handled better than wealth because it keeps us active, keeps us working. Poverty can unite a family that struggles together to make ends meet.

Though we were not poor, Jeannette and my children and I all worked together to make the Dwarf House a success. Dan and Bubba joined me in building Chick-fil-A, and Trudy has come alongside us in a wide range of ministries through our family's WinShape Foundation.

Our *Impossible Dream* was a penthouse condominium, but our greatest dream come true is the joy we share as a family united in our work and our purpose. And as long as that purpose remains larger than a piece of real estate or anything else we might want to purchase, we will stay strong as a family.

SHARE
WEALTH
GENEROUSLY

Our Highest Calling

Years ago, at Christmastime, I visited two brothers who lived at the Christian City children's home. I had a gift for each of them, but when I arrived, they were both so excited they could hardly contain themselves. They each handed me a present, which I opened: two small bottles of lotion they wanted me to have. They were so pleased to share their gift, and the joy almost overwhelmed them. Their joy filled my heart. They were experiencing their highest calling in life—to give—and they weren't even thinking about what I might have brought for them.

The whole world around us is a reminder to give. Why did God create trees? To give us shelter, fruit, timber, and oxygen. The ground, the stars, the moon, the cattle in the fields—all of them were created to give. Likewise, we were created to give. That's why we experience so much joy when we give generously.

If I were allowed only one answer to the

question, "Wealth, is it worth it?" it would be this: "Yes, if you give it generously."

Don't wait until you can afford it to start giving. Start right now enjoying that wonderful feeling we experience when we share our resources.

I began this book by writing about the inspiration of Warren Buffett and Bill Gates, who are giving away billions of dollars. They've been blessed with an incredible opportunity to make a difference through their giving. So have you and I. We don't have to give away a billion dollars to change the world. Sometimes a bottle of lotion is all it takes.

I'm going to close with the stories of people who didn't wait to become rich before they started giving generously. These people and their impact should be our inspiration. After all, when Jesus talked about giving, his most powerful example was not about a wealthy person giving from his wealth, but the poor widow who gave all she had.

Start giving. Right now!

The Safest Investment

I once had the opportunity to meet John Templeton, one of the most respected financial investors of the twentieth century. I had read a statement he had made regarding tithing, which is giving 10 percent of your earnings to your church (or charity). He said, "Most other investments have risk factors. But in my judgment, [thithing] is a sure thing."

When I met him, I asked him about that statement. He not only confirmed it, he added, "I've never known anyone who tithed for ten years and did not reap great benefits."

"Money Is Not the Main Motivator"

Richard and Stephanye Yadkowski had a choice. Richard had been a Chick-fil-A restaurant operator at a mall location for six years, and he had earned the opportunity to operate a stand-alone restaurant and greatly increase his income.

But for more than ten years, Richard and Stephanye had been telling me that they felt called to serve as house parents in a children's home—not a job known for high salaries—and they hoped for an opportunity at one of our WinShape foster homes. For all those years I encouraged them to focus on their own children and their marriage before considering the challenges of a foster home. Then in 2006 Richard told me he thought it was time. If we had an opening for house parents at any of our homes, he and Stephanye would like to apply for the position.

That's when I asked Richard, "If I could get you a stand-alone restaurant, would you rather do that?" Richard said no. The choice of significantly more income that I was offering was not a choice to them. They believed they had to follow God's calling.

"I didn't spend much time thinking about the offer," Richard says today. "Not because I didn't appreciate it. I was honored by your confidence in me. Becoming house parents was our purpose, our path in life. For many years we had searched this out and tested it, asking God, 'Are you sure?' We felt confident it was our path.

"We knew the world would not understand. People would think we're crazy for wanting to do this. It's tough to raise your own kids plus six extras from different backgrounds, some with serious issues, and to do that in lieu of having a large income. But when you love what you're doing and know it's what God created you for, then money is not the main motivator."

Beyond Anything
Money Can Buy

Richard and Stephanye's decision to become house parents and not operate a stand-alone Chick-fil-A restaurant was not surprising to me. Richard was thirteen years old when he became one of the first children to live at our first WinShape home. By that time he had already lived with seven other sets of foster parents. "Being bounced around, I learned from all of them and appreciate what they did," Richard says. "And for a long time I thought I never wanted to have children, because I was afraid I would do a terrible job and continue the cycle. So when Stephanye and I did have children, I was determined that my kids would never grow up in a foster home. Now that's exactly what they're doing—growing up in *our* foster home."

In fact, Richard and Stephanye are house parents in the very home Richard came to when he was thirteen. Doug and Julie Bowling, his house parents more than twenty years ago, are still serving in the WinShape home down the street. They are typical of the house parents at our twelve WinShape homes across the South. Each couple has responded to a calling by making a lifelong commitment to serving children. As Richard noted, that commitment is misunderstood by some, but the rewards are beyond anything money can buy.

Jeannette
has had a wonderful
relationship with our twelve
grandchildren throughout their
lives and has shared her
wisdom with them more times
than any of them could count.
"Grandmama's praying for
you," I've heard her say again
and again. "Be sure you
make good choices."

STC

Preparing Us for Opportunities

Hapeville, Georgia, where we opened the Dwarf House in 1946, was the home of the Georgia Baptist Children's Home, and I would pass by it going from my home to the restaurant. Whenever I saw children outside playing, or when some of them came to the restaurant for something to drink, I wondered about their circumstances—where they came from and what might have happened to their parents. It would be thirty years before I had the resources and the opportunity to open the first WinShape home. God prepares our hearts to use our resources to respond to the needs of those around us.

"We've Got to Do Something!"

We give most generously when we are passionate about a cause, and no cause makes us more passionate than our children, especially when they are hurting.

James Shepherd nearly died in an accident in 1973. He had just graduated from college and was backpacking in countries around the world. While in Brazil he was bodysurfing at the beach at Rio de Janeiro, and a wave slammed him to the bottom, instantly paralyzing him from the neck down. James was saved from the water and transported to a hospital. His parents, Alana and Harold, immediately flew to Brazil to be at his side in the hospital and during the early days of his recovery, then they looked for a place in the United States that offered treatment and rehabilitation from spinal cord injuries. The best fit for James was in Denver, Colorado, twelve hundred miles from home.

Weeks later, back in Atlanta, James and his parents thought about creating a spinal rehabilitation center in Atlanta so patients and families wouldn't have to travel so far for treatment. "We were so naive," Alana says. "We just said, 'Why not?' If we had seen the challenges lying ahead of us, we might have run the other direction."

Instead, Alana recalls, "It was like God saying to us, 'I have a mission for you.'"

The Shepherds and Dr. David Apple started with just six beds and a dream. "We had a model of an eighty-bed hospital, patterning ourselves after the hospital in Denver," Alana says.

Thirty-five years later, the Shepherd Spinal Center is ranked among the top ten rehabilitation hospitals in the United States. The 132-bed facility admits nearly a thousand people annually to its inpatient programs and more than five hundred people to its day-patient programs. Shepherd sees another six thousand people annually on an outpatient basis.

Financial Support of Many

F acilities as substantial as the Shepherd Center are not built by an individual or a single family. Many, many generous supporters join hands.

"When you start something like this hospital," Alana says, "your position or business in the community can be a stepping-stone or the rock you stand on."

For the Shepherds, that stepping-stone was Harold Shepherd's position of respect among highway contractors and related suppliers. Harold and his two brothers founded Shepherd Construction Company, one of Georgia's largest road construction companies. His colleagues in the industry responded to the Shepherds' call for financial assistance.

"And many of our friends have supported us generously," Alana says. "This is nothing we could have done with our financial resources alone. We needed a lot of community support to get to where we are. That support has allowed us to expand the hospital and to offer treatment to many patients who cannot pay. About one-third of our patients are in scholarship beds."

My friends laugh *and say, "If Alana comes in the room, you'd better watch your wallet." I hope I have a soft sell about encouraging people to donate their money. The Center wouldn't exist without them.*

ALANA SHEPHERD

$\mathcal{G}$iving $\mathcal{M}$ore than $\mathcal{M}$oney

T he Shepherds have given much more than their money. James Shepherd, who now uses a scooter because of his accident, serves as chairman of the board, and Alana is the chief fund-raiser. "This is my mission in life," Alana says. "This is my chance to do something to help others, and I can't turn my back on it. I've had the opportunity, because of my husband's business success, to work without receiving a salary. My compensation is the great feeling I receive every day—feelings of accomplishment, touching other people and having a part in other people's lives as they overcome obstacles."

When Alana talks about the opportunities she has missed by working full time long beyond any traditional retirement age, she briefly laments, "I haven't been as involved in the lives of my grown children as some of my friends have."

Then she recalls a friend who mentored in the early years of Shepherd. Be Haas was extremely successful in fund-raising and active into her nineties. "Be told me she was worried that nobody would come to her funeral because she didn't have time to keep up with her friends," Alana says. "That might or might not be the case, but you can get busy and get caught up in something that's worthwhile and meaningful."

She pauses and adds, "James says he often leaves the hospital in the afternoon with tears on his face—it's been such a privilege to be part of it. He's experienced such pain, and I've never seen him complain. It's truly amazing."

Alana leaves her office and walks down the hall, speaking with patients and staff all along the way. "Passion is such a part of this place," she says. "So many of our department heads and staff work here because they want to work here. We have very little turnover. They love the interaction with patients and families."

Just like Alana, Harold, and James Shepherd have for nearly forty years.

J.B. Fuqua Knew
the Joy of Giving

"Do you think we can live on three hundred dollars a month?"

That was the question J.B. Fuqua asked Dottie Chapman before he proposed marriage.

"I said, yes, of course," Dottie remembers, "and we did get married and live on three hundred dollars a month. But not for long. J.B. and I were both hard workers."

J.B. and Dottie Fuqua are not known today so much for their humble beginnings as for J.B.'s business success and their generous philanthropy. J.B. donated many millions of dollars before he passed away in 2006, and Dottie continues to give generously. In fact, J.B. once told me that the more he gave away, the more he seemed to get. In his later years he spent much of his time and effort giving money away. He had an office on the top floor of One Atlantic Center in Atlanta where he employed a staff to help him identify worthy recipients. Many people have benefited from his philanthropic efforts, including my wife, Jeannette, who had her pacemaker replaced at the Fuqua Heart Center at Piedmont Hospital. What a gratifying feeling to have that purpose in life!

J.B. especially enjoyed giving where he had a personal connection. When he was a teenager growing up in rural Virginia, Duke University allowed him borrow business books by mail. Decades later J.B. became one of Duke's largest benefactors. He also donated millions to rescue a school in his hometown of Farmville, Virginia, and transform it into a fine institution.

Dottie inspired his giving. She was, and remains, active in many civic causes, and she had to be careful when she discussed her interests with J.B. Because of his love for Dottie and his desire to support anything she was involved in, J.B. was quick to offer financial support to those causes. Many of J.B.'s gifts to the community were actually gifts to Dottie—love letters for all of us to see. Her love of flowers and involvement in the Atlanta Botanical Garden inspired J.B. to ensure the creation of the

Dorothy Chapman Fuqua Conservatory and later the adjacent Orchid House. Her concern for mental health issues resulted in significant support for Skyland Trail, community-based residential and day mental health treatment facility for adults with serious mental illness in Atlanta.

I could see how much J.B. enjoyed giving. Whenever we got together, our conversations rarely began with business. He had more fun talking about the opportunities he had been given to share his wealth. And he wanted to give away as much as possible while he was alive to see the impact.

Life at the Rock Ranch

I wish I had as much fun as Jeff Manley does. Jeff's job is to make sure everybody around is having a good time. What could be better than that? Jeff is always smiling, always up, always pouring out his energy for the enjoyment of others. He gives and gives and gives, and I think that giving is the source of his joy.

Jeff has transformed the Rock Ranch, a working cattle ranch I bought years ago, into a fun destination for thousands of people who come to get lost in a corn maze, take hayrides and pony rides, camp in a Conestoga wagon, ride the cow train, see hot-air balloons and Fourth of July fireworks, watch pumpkins get thrown across a field by a giant slingshot, drive through a mile-long Christmas lights show, go fishing, ride paddle boats, and much, much more. Every time I see him, he tells me about another idea he has.

Jeff calls what he does "agritourism," a combination of agriculture and tourism. I just call it a fun way to give to others.

Talent for Making People Smile

W hen my children were growing up, I would take them to the Rock Ranch for cattle sales—our own brand of low-key fun that gave us all special memories. When I bought the ranch, however, it had been out of operation for years. The owner had passed away, and his family called and asked if I would be interested in purchasing it. Of course, I was. It's easy to get caught up in the dream of becoming a cattle rancher.

We had just hired Jeff Manley to help start Camp WinShape, a summer camp for girls and boys on the Berry College campus in north Georgia. I had known Jeff since he was twelve years old and working in a Jonesboro drugstore. He was a hard worker, the kind of man who could get a tired ranch going in the right direction. He agreed to help me with the ranch instead of working at WinShape, and just like that, I was in the cattle business.

Jeff operated it somewhat successfully—he even served as an officer in the Cattlemen's Association—

but even a successful cattle ranch struggles to make a profit. So when people started asking Jeff if they could have picnics at the ranch or bring their company out for a day, Jeff had a vision for transforming the Rock Ranch into a place where families could experience God's creation with outings, special events, and themed events over several weekends in October and November.

He cut a maze in a cornfield, brought in singers and bluegrass musicians, invited everybody to join in hillbilly karaoke, arm wrestling, and lawnmower racing. He had a tug-of-war with ranch hands Henry and Max taking on everyone else in attendance at the same time. Then there was Pumpkin Destruction Day, with a pumpkin cannon, pumpkin bowling, the hammer smash, and the lift-crane pumpkin drop. If that wasn't enough, there was a falconry demonstration, birds of prey exhibition, archery, fishing rodeo, insect education lab, wildlife station, and a reptile show.

Jeff has a God-given talent for making people smile. "The goal at the Rock Ranch is to create an opportunity for families to spend quality time together and provide educational and entertaining programs that create positive life memories," Jeff says. "Throughout the years, we've learned to blend our love of agriculture with entertainment to keep people interested and involved in a way of life that our grandparents knew well but now is in danger of being forgotten."

Of course, we still raise cattle—the experience wouldn't be authentic if we didn't—but we like the smiles most of all.

Giving Children Peace at the Rock

The timing of our purchase of the Rock Ranch coincided with God's calling us to open foster homes for children. I couldn't imagine a better place for children to grow up. Our own children had grown up on a farm, chasing cattle in the fields, running down to the river, or riding motorbikes all over the place. I often recall one special Saturday many years ago. I had set aside the whole day to spend with Dan, Bubba, and Trudy, and I took them to a horse show and then to The Varsity for lunch. After lunch we went to a show, and we all walked back to the car a little tired but satisfied with a good day.

We were driving home to the farm, and I could hear the children talking in the back of the station wagon. After a few minutes they asked me, "Daddy, next Saturday can we stay home all day long?"

I had to smile. I had planned a big day on the town for them, and they were just as happy, maybe more so, at the thought of staying on the farm, where they could run down to the river or create their own games.

The Rock Ranch could offer that same kind of peaceful wide-open space for children to grow up.

The vision for special events at the Rock was all Jeff's. He understood my desire for children in our foster homes to grow up in the setting of a working ranch, and so he created those opportunities for families to enjoy those experiences. Anybody can take pleasure in the beauty of a large working ranch for a day. Children who have grown up in the city can sit around a bonfire and sleep overnight in covered wagons.

I especially enjoy the special Saturday events, like the Fourth of July and our Fall Family Fun Days. It's very rewarding to me to see so many families with little children trailing behind them at the outing, experiencing God's wonderful creation.

If you have
real character, money will
not spoil it. Persons with
genuine character can handle
adversity and prosperity.

STC

Deen Day Sanders Reflects on Wealth and "God With Us"

N early fifteen years after my family and I moved out of the nation's first government housing project, Cecil and Deen Day moved into an apartment there at Techwood Homes with their two children and a third on the way. It was the 1950s, and Cecil was a student on the G.I. Bill at nearby Georgia Tech. He also had a job at Sears and worked part-time as a draftsman for Moncrief Heating and Air Conditioning. Deen sold greeting cards door to door to supplement their income.

With that kind of work schedule, they didn't plan to stay long at Techwood Homes. In fact, Cecil and Deen became two of Atlanta's most successful and generous business leaders. In 1970 Cecil founded Days Inns of America, a lodging chain that grew from start-up to three hundred locations in just eight years. Cecil died of cancer in 1978, and Deen became chairman of the

Investment Company as well as the Cecil B. Day Foundation and became a business partner.

As Deen, who is now married to James Sanders, looks back on the incredible financial changes her family experienced with the creation and growth of Days Inn, she reflects on the question, Wealth, is it worth it? Her observations highlight the constants in their life:

Cecil and I were always content regardless of where we were living. We were never possessed by our possessions. We knew that contentment is not found in things.

We always set goals.

We always tithed and gave back to the Lord's work 10 percent of our income. When we were living at Techwood Homes, we took an old box with a slit in the top and put our change in it. It was amazing that when we counted it out, we would have our tithe.

We had just as many friends when we were living at Techwood Homes as we did later as owners of Days Inns. In fact, we have kept the same friends through the years.

We always understood that it is important to remember that everything we have is a gift from God and we have to use the gifts in a responsible way.

God's providential hand works with us and guides us. He goes before us. I ask God what plan He has for my life, but I don't sit around begging for guidance. I know He is working that out. Emmanuel is my favorite name for Jesus. "God with Us."

We have to be willing vessels—to be willing to seek and follow God's plan for our lives.

Years ago, when leading a group through Henry Blackaby's workbook, Experiencing God, *I learned to look at what God is already doing and partner with that work. I learned to pray that God would give me the vision and discernment where and how to invest in the eternal.*

Wealth should not be used for self-aggrandizement.

We did not seek elitism, which comes in many forms, such as intellectualism, based on degrees from various institutions, more knowledge of the Bible than others, property in prestigious locations, or economic control of others. Wealth opens doors for all of the above. But, when you use it for selfish purposes, it is self-centered and borders on idolatry. Wealth should be used to serve others as often as possible and to serve the Lord for His glory in every way possible.

Wealth is a blessing if you invest in things that have eternal consequences and results.

When you read about Deen's philosophy on wealth, it's probably not surprising to learn that she is helping to guide young people to a better understanding of the power and the attraction of wealth. At Georgia Tech, she has funded the Cecil B. Day Chair in Business Ethics. "Cecil Day was an intelligent, successful businessman," Deen says, "but more important, he was an honest, ethical man. Students need to understand that you don't have to make a choice between success and ethics."

Counting Our Blessings

E very year Chick-fil-A brings together restaurant franchisee operators and spouses from around the country for a seminar, and we report on the progress of the chain, discuss plans for the future, and offer training opportunities. Our time together becomes like a family reunion where we share our joys and our trials.

In 2010 we met in Washington, D.C., and were reminded of the difficult times many people in our nation were experiencing. We all were familiar with terms such as business failures and bankruptcies, foreclosures and joblessness. Restaurant operators told one another stories of customers and friends who were experiencing extremely tough times—the worst some had ever experienced.

Dr. Charles Carter, my pastor, opened our seminar by reminding us that we were not given guarantees of good times. To illustrate, he pointed to King David, who in his most difficult days wrote a series of psalms about being sick and miserable, burning with fever, and surrounded by enemies in a land of exile. Yet in the middle of this these psalms of misery, he inserted a song of praise, uplift, and delight. He wrote that the Lord lifted him out of the slimy pit, set him on a firm place to stand, and put a new song in his mouth: "Many, Lord my God, are the wonders you have done for us" (Psalm 40:5, NIV).

In other words, David is counting his blessings.

"That's my challenge to us," Charles said. "When people are talking about the tough times, the difficult times, let's remember how wonderfully we are blessed." Then he recited a song I've sung so many times since I was a boy:

Count your many blessings, name them one by one
Count your many blessings, see what God hath done!
Count your many blessings, name them one by one,
And it will surprise you what the Lord hath done.

It sounds so simple, but if we will count our blessings and remember the source of our blessings—when we see wealth as a gift and we pledge to be faithful stewards of that gift—then our wealth will indeed be worth it.

$\mathcal{A}$fterword

Dr. Charles Q. Carter

W hen people learn that I was Truett Cathy's pastor for twenty-seven years, they often ask, "Is Truett for real? Is he really as generous as he is portrayed?"

My answer is an emphatic yes, but the truth is much more complex.

No question is more relevant to a person's character and integrity than how one deals with material possessions. As Truett writes, and we have seen, wealth is notorious for ruining people who otherwise were of good moral character. So it was not without reason that Jesus warned about riches and the difficulty of a rich man entering the kingdom of God, or heaven. The path to authentic wealth, true riches, and abundant living, Jesus explained, is through giving: "Sell your possessions and give to the poor" (Matthew 19:21). And he reserved the strong word fool for the farmer who thought more about building bigger barns to store his harvest rather than feeding the hungry.

I met Truett in 1973, long before he became wealthy by the world's standards. In those days he was a successful small businessman still building his company. What impressed me then and now was that he always practiced generous giving, in most cases anonymously. Many times through the years Truett has asked me to serve as a go-between, allowing him to make an anonymous donation. In many of those cases he was not so concerned about whether he was recognized, but rather that the recipients were not embarrassed or humiliated by their unfortunate position.

As pastor to Truett and Jeannette from 1973 until I retired in 2000, I watched Chick-fil-A grow into a national brand with more than $1 billion in sales. All the while the Cathys' self-perception remained constant. Truett took his Sunday school teaching position seriously, seldom missing a Sunday with his thirteen-year-old boys class. And

Jeannette was always a faithful member of her Sunday school class and our church choir. As pastor I often observed Truett in worship, usually with young people sitting with him and sometimes sharing a hymnal with someone whom I knew had recently lost his job.

Truett embodies the truth of Rudyard Kipling's words: If you can walk with kings and not lose the common touch. I was with Truett shortly after he learned that he would be listed among *Forbes* magazine's 400 richest people in American, the titans of American commerce. While most people would be pleased and proud to see their name on such a list, Truett was concerned by the message the listing might send. He did not like the characterization of himself as rich, and he wondered how *Forbes* came up with its estimate of his net worth, since Chick-fil-A is not a publicly traded company. Truett would rather talk about where he has come from than where he is. He would rather talk about his mother's hard work running a boardinghouse during the Great Depression or the joy he experienced while working for twenty-one years behind the counter of the Dwarf House restaurant before he opened the first Chick-fil-A restaurant.

He was and remains a man blessed with a remarkable idea, a unique ability to recognize the opportunities and pitfalls of a business deal, a discerning eye for recognizing talent, and a soft heart.

Truett's reputation—his good name—as a kind, compassionate, Christian gentleman sometimes leaves the impression that he is an easy touch for handouts. Not so. Among his many personal gifts is his uncanny ability to read people and identify their motives. There is no need for undeserving beggars to attempt to put him on a guilt trip if he has refused their appeal. Some believe they will sway his decision in their direction if they tell Truett, "God told me to ask you to buy me a car... build me a house...etc." This tactic almost always backfires, and Truett typically responds, "Well, God hasn't told me to do that just yet."

While the Cathys have given away much of their wealth, it would be inaccurate to say that Truett and Jeannette have taken vows of poverty.

They still insist on living a simple lifestyle in the same farmhouse they purchased in 1956, along with 262 acres of land, a tractor, and a few cows. They still greet visitors warmly at the kitchen door. But Truett often expresses gratitude for the privilege of enjoying what he calls the "extras" in life. He collects classic cars and Remington sculptures, and he has bought no small amount of real estate in Florida and Georgia. All of these things find their rightful place in Truett's hands, not his heart, which he reserves for his Lord, his family, his friends, and those in need, particularly children. The Cathys' *Impossible Dream* condominium, which Truett writes about, illustrates my point.

Years ago, Truett and Jeannette purchased a condominium unit in New Smyrna Beach, Florida, where they visit regularly. Through the years they have taken the opportunity to buy additional units, which they enjoy sharing with others.

In 2010 they bought the beautiful two-story penthouse unit after the price had fallen dramatically, but they do not stay there. They are more comfortable in a modest unit several floors below.

In the late afternoon, however, Jeannette and Truett go up to the penthouse to watch the sun set over the marsh and the moon rise from the Atlantic Ocean, marveling at God's wonderful creation.

Is Truett for real? He absolutely is!

I accomplished great things. I built myself houses and planted vineyards. I planted gardens and orchards, with all kinds of fruit trees in them; I dug ponds to irrigate them. I bought many slaves, and there were slaves born in my household. I owned more livestock than anyone else who had ever lived in Jerusalem. I also piled up silver and gold from the royal treasuries of the lands I ruled. Men and women sang to entertain me, and I had all the women a man could want.

Yes, I was great, greater than anyone else who had ever lived in Jerusalem, and my wisdom never failed me. Anything I wanted, I got. I did not deny myself any pleasure. I was proud of everything I had worked for, and all this was my reward. Then I thought about all that I had done and how hard I had worked doing it, and I realized that it didn't mean a thing. It was like chasing the wind, of no use at all.

ECCLESIASTES 2:4-11

After all this, there is only one thing to say: Have reverence for God, and obey his commands, because this is all that we were created for. God is going to judge everything we do, whether good or bad, even things done in secret.

ECCLESIASTES 12:13-14